W9-CRO-199

I'M AN AMERICAN CITIZEN

Our Country's Holidays

Janice Charleston

PowerKiDS press™

NEW YORK

Published in 2013 by The Rosen Publishing Group, Inc.
29 East 21st Street, New York, NY 10010

Book Design: Katelyn Londino

Photo Credits: Cover TIMOTHY A. CLARY/Staff/AFP/Getty Images; p. 4 Ariel Skelley/Photographer's Choice/Getty Images; p. 5 Digital Vision/Thinkstock.com; p. 6 Hulton Archive/Stringer/Archive Photos/Getty Images; pp. 7, 11, 15 (fireworks) iStockphoto/Thinkstock.com; p. 8 commons.wikimedia.org/wiki/File:Stuart-george-washington-constable-1797.jpg/Wikipedia.org; p. 9 Boykov/Shutterstock.com; p. 10 ©iStockphoto.com/jbrizendine; p. 12 Brandon Jennings/Shutterstock.com; p. 13 Gianna Stadelmyer/Shutterstock.com; p. 14 KidStock/Blend Images/Getty Images; p. 15 (parade) Frances L Fruit/Shutterstock.com; p. 16 Kurhan/Shutterstock.com; p. 17 commons.wikimedia.org/wiki/File:Christopher_Columbus.PNG/Wikipedia.org; p. 18 Tim Bieber/Lifesize/Getty Images; p. 19 Anthony Correia/Shutterstock.com; p. 20 Photodisc/Thinkstock.com; p. 21 Comstock/Thinkstock.com.

Library of Congress Cataloging-in-Publication Data

Charleston, Janice.
Our country's holidays / Janice Charleston.
    p. cm. — (I'm an American citizen)
Includes index.
ISBN 978-1-4488-8833-7 (pbk.)
ISBN 978-1-4488-8834-4 (6-pack)
ISBN 978-1-4488-8587-9 (library binding)
1. Holidays—United States—Juvenile literature. I. Title.
GT4803.C47 2013
394.26973—dc23

                    2012010989

Manufactured in the United States of America

CPSIA Compliance Information: Batch #WS12RC: For further information contact Rosen Publishing, New York, New York at 1-800-237-9932.

Word Count: 400

Contents

Time to Celebrate

It's fun to **celebrate** holidays. In the United States, we celebrate many holidays during the year. National holidays are holidays we celebrate as a whole country.

Americans celebrate holidays for different reasons.
Some holidays honor important people. Some holidays
celebrate important events.

Important Leaders

In January, we celebrate Martin Luther King Day.

Martin Luther King Jr. was an important leader.

He fought for a better life for African Americans.

On Martin Luther King Day, we celebrate what he taught us. He taught us to treat everyone fairly even if they're different from us.

Presidents' Day is in February. We celebrate George Washington's birthday on this day. He was America's first president.

On Presidents' Day, we honor all our presidents.

We celebrate the lives of our country's leaders.

Memorial Day

Memorial Day is in May. On this day, we honor **soldiers** who died while fighting in wars for our country.

We do special things on Memorial Day to honor
these soldiers. You can see many American flags on
Memorial Day.

Celebrating Our Freedom

We also see lots of American flags on June 14. This is Flag Day. The American flag is red, white, and blue. It has 13 stripes and 50 stars.

On Flag Day, we celebrate what the flag means to us.

The flag stands for our country and our **freedom**.

The flag is very important to Americans.

We celebrate America's birthday on the Fourth of July.

This holiday is also called Independence Day.

"Independence" means freedom.

On the Fourth of July, people go to **parades** and listen to songs about America. They watch fireworks, too. Fireworks are colorful and loud!

Honoring Workers

Labor Day is a special holiday in September. It celebrates American workers. On this day, we honor them for the hard work they do.

A Great Explorer

In October, we celebrate Columbus Day. This day is named after Christopher Columbus. He was an **explorer** who came to North America in 1492.

November Holidays

Veterans Day is on November 11. We honor all American soldiers on this day. It's a day to thank them for fighting for our country.

There are many parades on Veterans Day. We go
to these parades to honor soldiers from the past
and the present.

We celebrate Thanksgiving in November, too. We
show thanks for our family and friends. We also show
thanks for the food we eat.

Your Favorite Holiday

We have lots of things to celebrate in our country.

What's your **favorite** holiday? How do you celebrate it?

A Year of Holidays

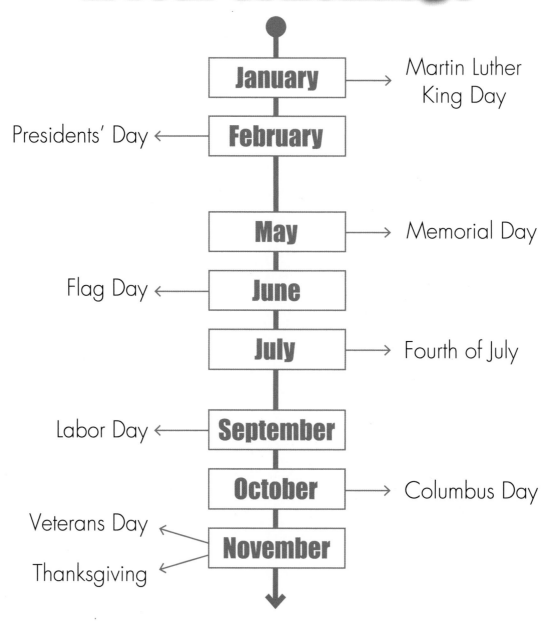

January → Martin Luther King Day

Presidents' Day ← February

May → Memorial Day

Flag Day ← June

July → Fourth of July

Labor Day ← September

October → Columbus Day

Veterans Day ← November

Thanksgiving ←

Glossary

celebrate (SEH-luh-brayt) To do special things for a holiday or other important day.

explorer (ihk-SPLOHR-uhr) Someone who travels to find new places.

favorite (FAY-vuh-ruht) Liked best.

freedom (FREE-duhm) When a person or group is free.

parade (puh-RAYD) An event where people walk in the streets and bands play music.

soldier (SOHL-juhr) A person who fights for their country in a war.

Index

Due to the changing nature of Internet links, The Rosen Publishing Group, Inc., has developed an online list of websites related to the subject of this book. This site is updated regularly. Please use this link to access the list: **www.powerkidslinks.com/iac/holi**